OUT OF THE WAY
GOURMET

DISCOVERING THE HIDDEN GEMS OF THE MAINE FOOD SCENE

RONNI ARNO and
VERONICA STUBBS

Down East Books

Published by Down East Books
An imprint of Globe Pequot
Trade division of The Rowman & Littlefield
Publishing Group, Inc.
4501 Forbes Blvd., Ste. 200
Lanham, MD 20706
www.rowman.com
www.downeastbooks.com

Distributed by NATIONAL BOOK NETWORK
Copyright © 2023 by Ronni Arno and Veronica Stubbs
All photographs provided by the establishments featured
in this book.

Interior design by Lynda Chilton, Chilton Creative

ISBN 978-1-68475-055-9 (paperback)
ISBN 978-1-68475-056-6 (e-book)

∞™ The paper used in this publication meets the minimum
requirements of American National Standard for Information
Sciences—Permanence of Paper for Printed Library Materials,
ANSI/NISO Z39.48-1992.

❦ Contents ❧

Authors' Note

We love Maine. The diverse landscapes (we boast bold ocean, island-dotted bays, and glorious snow-capped mountains), the close-knit community (it's often said that Maine is one big, small town), and the food (which is why we wrote this book). We all know that Portland has recently been rated one of the best cities in the country for foodies, but Maine's fabulous food scene extends far beyond Cumberland County. There are tiny, sometimes hidden food gems throughout the state, and this book will help you find them.

Just as important as the food, though, are the people who create it. We wanted to find out not only how these folks came up with these little hidden gems, but why. We met people who wanted to share the culinary delights from their home countries, people whose fans provided them with a brand new oven so they could continue baking for their community, and even people whose love of food started with tragedy.

The food you'll read about is spectacular, there's no doubt about that! Your mouth will water and you may find yourself jumping into your car to follow the routes of where to find made-from-scratch waffles with real Maine blueberry compote, crispy, thin-crust pizza fresh out of the oven and topped with basil straight from the garden, or sweet and gooey maple-glazed cinnamon rolls.

But what we found through these stories transcends food. We found Mainers. Mainers who come from all over the globe to share their culinary talents and often-unique creations. And we hope this book will help you find them, too.

Keep in mind that many of these amazing folks are not open year-round, or even every day during the busy season. And even if they are, they sometimes unexpectedly close for a myriad of reasons; their granddaughter is starring in a school play, there is a severe snowstorm, or simply because it's a perfect beach day. Please call ahead or check online to be sure your favorite spot is open on the day you plan to visit.

We hope you love the stories, the food, and the folks who make them as much as we do. We thought it would be appropriate to start your journey with our own Veronica Stubbs (the only story told in first-person), who shares her tale of how she came to Maine and started The Scone Goddess, which was the catalyst for writing this book. If Veronica could create a business out of her passion for baking, how many other folks out there did the same?

You're about to find out. Enjoy the ride and arrive hungry!

With love,
Ronni Arno & Veronica Stubbs

The Scone Goddess

Veronica Stubbs
1390 Atlantic Hwy
NORTHPORT

In December of 2016 my family and I left Vermont for the call of the ocean. Seduced by the sea air, friendly faces, and slower pace of life, our family was thrilled to call Northport home.

After moving to Maine, I found employment with a local company that kept me busy but did not fulfill my need to be with my community. Having had a successful bed and breakfast in Vermont that featured my 5-star breakfast, I knew that utilizing my skills in the kitchen would be a way to connect with new friends and neighbors. I went through the process of licensing my home kitchen so that I could bake my delicious treats at home for the local farmer's market each Saturday. Reflecting on how popular the scones were at the B & B, I decided baking scones would be the best way to earn some extra money and meet my new community. In years past, a friend had tasted my scones and exclaimed, "You are a scone goddess!" Remembering that story brought a smile to my face, so a banner was made (which was a Farmer's Market requirement), naming my home-based business "The Scone Goddess."

Each Saturday found me awake before dawn, baking

hundreds of scones: wild Maine blueberry, raspberry & cream, apple cinnamon, turtle, triple chocolate, and pumpkin scones. If you can dream it, I can make it! I also offered cute little tin-tied coffee bags with my scone mix so that people could enjoy baking fresh warm scones at home. The business quickly gained a following and I started to sell out at the market. The success enabled me to leave my full-time job and just bake scones for the market and a few local businesses. It was rather surreal! I had no idea so many people liked scones!

The pandemic forced many businesses to pivot, and The Scone Goddess was no different. The Farmer's Market closed, and I lost the majority of the fresh baked scones clientele. Rather than wait out the pandemic, I expanded the variety

of scone mixes offered and created a website. People's need to keep occupied while we were all shut in at home created a whole new generation of bakers. With groceries limited, buying online was a great way to try something new for these home bakers experimenting in their kitchens. This caused The Scone Goddess website sales to take off sooner than expected. Never anticipating the demand for scones, I had always hand mixed my recipe in ten-gallon buckets, then my daughter and I would hand-bag-and-seal the premium mixes.

Barely able to keep up with demand, I realized that more space and a faster way to get the product manufactured was needed. I invested in food grade cement mixers and a vibratory weigh/fill machine. This improvement allowed me to be able to produce 600 bags a day with just a two-person team.

Still working from home and having expanded to our newly renovated garage, dubbed, "The Production Room," I reached out to retailers and offered the premium scone mixes for wholesale. Heading into year two of owning The Scone Goddess, I realized that I'd better get serious. What was once a fun way to meet the community had turned into quite a little business. Staff was hired and The Scone Goddess was trademarked.

The pandemic had started to pause as the summer of 2021 rolled in, so I had a custom food trailer built and wrapped in The Scone Goddess logo. We lived in the tiniest out-of-the-way town, but were lucky that busy Route 1 ran right through it. The fresh baked scones trailer opened for business in May of that year with the support of my friend Liz, owner of The Bayside Store in Northport. Having a place to park the food trailer on Route 1 was really great for brand

exposure and allowed me to see
if there was enough scone love
to support a brick and mortar
in the town. After selling out
in fifteen minutes, almost
daily, I knew I was on the right
track with The Scone Goddess!

December 3rd of 2021,
my team opened The Scone
Goddess Little Scone Cottage
in Northport. The dream of
a life in Maine with a community of friends had become
reality. Along the way, I found
that my passion for baking and
community made a really fun
business.

———◦◆◦———

OPEN YEAR ROUND
Tuesday thru Saturday
7:30 a.m. to Noon
207-505-0004

She Grows Farm

Featured at Renew ME Day Spa
39 Main Street
BELFAST

Manis, Pedis, Pie? You read that correctly! Belfast, Maine has always been known as an artsy, quirky town. So it should not come as any surprise that you will find the most delicious pies for sale at a Day Spa & Beauty Boutique on Main Street. Definitely worth a look, the Renew ME Spa offers a pie cooler from She Grows Farm, filled with delicious pies for every season, with wild Maine blueberry stealing the show!

Kathy Strickland, married into the family that once owned the Jackson Bakery of Belfast, had never really been a pie maker. But she did love to pick fresh strawberries from her farm, She Grows Farm, and sell them by the roadside on Route 1. When her husband Ken had a powerful craving for strawberry pie, Kathy whipped one up from his family's pie recipe. It was just as delicious as Ken imagined it would be, and with his rave reviews, their friends also asked Kathy to make them pies. Before she knew it, Karthy was making strawberry pies to sell on Route 1 alongside her fresh fruit.

Kathy's friends and family thought that she should really do more with pies. After mastering her in-laws' family

recipes, Kathy now bakes pies in her licensed home kitchen and delivers them to the spa that her daughters own. "We are actually fourth generation pie makers now," Kathy says. "My daughter Kendra helps make pies with me." In fact, Kendra was making pies with her mom when she went into labor with her third child. "I felt a little weird," Kendra remembers. "but I kept baking until it was time to head home. I was so busy that I didn't even realize that my water broke and I had been in labor!" Of course, they gifted the labor nurses with pie after the birth of Kendra's daughter.

The most expensive pie they ever sold was a whopping $80! Shortly after starting to sell the pies at the spa in 2021, a woman and her husband came in and tried a slice of blueberry.

"The husband told me he didn't even like blueberry pie," Kathy says, "but that this blueberry pie was fantastic!" They then bought another entire pie to take with them. After the couple returned home to North Carolina, the woman called Kathy and insisted that

she ship her a blueberry pie. "I let her know that blueberry pie just does not ship well," Kathy says, "but the customer insisted." Using shrink wrap to secure the pie, Kathy carefully packaged it and shipped it to North Carolina at the shipping cost of $60! The pie arrived mashed, but a good mashed pie is still a tasty mashed pie.

She Grows Farm takes special orders by calling the spa, or by stopping in, in person, for those lucky enough to know about this hidden little secret.

⊃·◆·⊂

OPEN YEAR ROUND
Monday, Noon to 5:00 p.m.
Tuesday thru Friday, 9:00 a.m. to 5:00 p.m.
Saturday, 10:00 a.m. to 5:00 p.m.
207-356-8063

Jamaican Grille

37 Front St.
(behind the Front Street Pub)
BELFAST

ocated at the back of the Front Street Pub but only accessible from the Belfast Harborwalk, Jamaican Grille uses approximately 12 by 15 square feet of kitchen space to make authentic, mouth-watering, melt-off-the-bone jerk chicken, pork ribs, and steak tips.

"People always ask how a white guy wound up serving Jamaican food in the middle of the harborwalk in Midcoast Maine," says owner Eldon (Jason) Loblein. "The inspiration for this place goes back to my experiences spending time as a kid in Rose Garden, Long Bay, Jamaica, which is about thirty minutes away from the origin of jerk chicken."

Born and raised in Belfast, Jason's family spent several months out of each year in Jamaica.

Jason's father, a

builder, would work in Belfast for half the year, and then go to Jamaica for the remainder of the year. "I was probably about five or six the first time we went," Jason says. "We lived on the quiet side of the island in a village, and we were the only white family in that area." Jason loved to spend time with the neighbor kids, who often came from farming families. A curious child, Jason would go next door on Sundays and watch the neighbor's families slaughter goats for cooking. "The families were so generous," Jason says. "Everybody feeds each other. They always wanted to share food, even if it was a big plate of rice with just a little meat and gravy."

Ricardo Benjamin, Jason's neighbor at the time, helped his grandfather to make jerk seasoning using ingredients from the nearby mountains. As a member of the community, neighbors become like family, and culture and cooking become naturally absorbed. "Whenever I went to someone's house, if they were cooking, I was asked to participate," Jason says. He was often handed a knife with instructions to cut the chicken. "I learned how to make a fire, I learned how to cook over a fire, and I learned how to prep the meat. I learned pretty quickly that food always tastes better cooked over fire."

In 2002, Jason decided to set up a grill in downtown Belfast, in front of a friend's shop. He started with a 55-gallon drum and a little grill with charcoal and a pot of oil, and only sold jerk chicken with festival. Festival, it turns out, is a deep-fried cornbread, and it's currently on Jamaican Grille's menu as "deep-fried cornbread," to avoid the inevitable question: What is festival?

Shortly after opening his grill, Jason started college for music in Florida, although he's also interested in art and programming. "The way that a recipe comes together is similar to how a song, or a piece of art, or even a website, come together," Jason says. "All of these require experimentation to create an ensemble, whether it be musical instruments, paint colors, or recipes. And then, the discipline comes in from going back and refining these things to make them better."

While in school, he decided to purchase a food truck that he would run in the summers. He found one formerly owned by the Maine Department of Defense, designed to be a mobile power and refrigeration unit in case of a nuclear fallout. After spray painting the truck with rasta colors, Jason named the truck "Jamaican Grille," and, with his friends Tim Wry and Anthony Jacovino, spent the summers cooking jerk chicken at outdoor fairs, music festivals, and lavish parties.

Five years later, the food truck closed, and Jason headed to California for a programming job (Tim would later establish Wry Design, a custom cabinet and furniture company, and Anthony would open Delvino's, a classy Italian eatery on Main Street in Belfast). "I was always stuck on a computer," Jason says. "So I spent quite a bit of time daydreaming about how I could open the Grille again, but make it better."

After contemplating how to streamline the process of cooking jerk chicken while still letting it cook over fire for that authentic Jamaican taste, Jason had a viable plan. Using his knowledge of technology, Jason figured out how to make the process faster without compromising on flavor and authenticity. "We have all the recipes written down in a book labled The Holy Bible," Jason says. "Every recipe is written down exactly as it should be prepared, with precise measurements of grams and milligrams and cooking time and temperature, so that the food can be prepared by any of our employees and still taste the same and are one-hundred percent replicable."

"The end goal of Jamaican Grille is to be the fast food name for Jamaican food and jerk chicken," Jason says. "When you think of fast food burgers, you think of McDonald's. When you think of fast food Mexican, you think of Chipotle. I'd love for Jamaican Grille to be known as the fast food for jerk chicken."

The menu is simple and reliable. The customer has a choice of jerk chicken, jerk pork ribs, or jerk steak tips. They then add their choice of sides, which include coconut rice and beans, deep-fried cornbread (aka festival), or a sweet and tangy vegetable mix of cabbage and carrots. Finally, they can add their choice of sauces, which include mild honey BBQ, lemon habanero, or superhot mango. A la carte items are also available for purchase, and the Jamaican Grille offers specials (like braised oxtail with butter beans and curry goat over rice) on occasion.

Jamaican Grille is usually open from April through the end of November. Since there's no indoor seating, the shop slows down when people can't eat outside. Jason is hoping that Portland will be the next location for Jamaican Grille, and will spend some time scouting out possible locations.

Jason works hard to ensure that his kitchen is a

low-stress, fun, and easy-as-possible atmosphere. Kitchen staff joke around while they work, but they stay true to Jason's recipes, making sure every dish is made exactly as it was when Jason was a child in Jamaica.

———◦•◆•◦———

OPEN LATE APRIL THRU EARLY NOVEMBER
Wednesday thru Sunday, 11:00 a.m. to 8:00 p.m.
207-323-1078

Toddy Pond Farm

174 Carver Road
MONROE

Located in rural Monroe lies 500 acres of lush farmland where grass-fed cattle, squealing piglets and energetic goats provide both the visual and gastric entertainment for the traveling foodie.

Greg and Heide Purinton-Brown have created a lovely escape from the crazy day-to-day. The ambiance created by live music, the company of the animals, and the amazing smell of food perfectly prepared is just the surface of this working farm. Greg and Heide farm with intention. After years in the corporate banking world, Greg told the *Ellsworth American* in 2015, "Being outdoors, working with animals and the land, improving a place and learning to adapt to all that nature has to offer; both challenging and rewarding, are all parts of what make farming so enjoyable for me." The cows raised for beef are grassfed on the lush organic fields. Calves stay with their mothers and gain nutrients from their mother's milk, as nature intended, rather than via a bottle. The lactating cows are only then milked once a day to retain the extra rich fat and nutrients that their milk has to offer. The farmers do not irrigate or till the land in order to minimize the impact on the surrounding environment. Heide says, "We believe farming should be a partnership with the land, mother nature, and the animals we share our farm with."

As the large barn twinkles with strings of lights hung from its rustic beams, live music spills into the rooms of the barn and out to the children who find wonder in the frolicking farm animals. Hot bubbling cheese and hand made sausage can be found sizzling on a crisp wood fired pizza. Cold hard cider pairs well with the perfectly spiced, slow roasted pork tacos, roasted steaks, or smoked meats. The meal is finished off with crisp vegetables and local brews.

Be sure to reserve your space in advance. The many entertainment acts and varying dinner menus sell out quickly. This complete Maine farm experience will be a fond memory that bears repeating year after year.

OPEN SEASONALLY

Friday & Saturday dinners by reservation only.
Reservations available at: toddypondfarm.com/farm-dinners
207-249-3344

STONE FOX CREAMERY

398 E Main St
SEARSPORT

Stone Fox Creamery gets the award for the richest ice cream around. So creamy with so little air added to their ice cream, a small dish of this premium dessert made with the finest ingredients is sure to satisfy you.

OPEN YEAR ROUND

Sunday thru Thursday, Noon to 6:00 p.m.
Friday thru Saturday, Noon to 7:00 p.m.
207-323-2850

Friar's Brewhouse Taproom

84A Main Street
BUCKSPORT

The entire town of Bucksport is a hidden gem, as travelers are so excited to get to Bar Harbor that they do not make plans to stop. Don't make this mistake! The town is full of delicious food, quaint shops and art galleries. Be sure to park and visit, and don't miss the tiny storefront that is Friar's Brewhouse Taproom. This humble establishment is home to the finest food and the most engaging hosts.

Friar's Brewhouse Taproom opened in 2018 by Brothers Donald Paul and Kenneth Leo, members of the Franciscan Brothers of St. Elizabeth of Hungary, twenty years after running the Friars' Bakehouse, a well-loved bakery, in Bangor. The brothers had a passion—and a knack—for bread-baking, which they used to create a gathering spot where people could be nourished, both in their stomachs and in their spirits. The brothers eventually decided to open a place closer to the monastery, where they could also include Brother Donald's passion for brewing beer. Beers range from classic German-style lagers to the brewery's best-selling whoopie pie porter.

The taproom is more than just a brewery. Brother Donald derives great pleasure in creating a meal that transcends taste and becomes an experience. Customers should arrive hungry, as the Friars are very generous with both their time and their portions. The restaurant features Brother Donald's famous Canadian pork pie, made with his mother's own special recipe for Quebec ketchup, Maine lobster rolls on homemade,

crusty, foot-long bread, and Bahn Mi, made with succulent slices of pork, tangy authentic Vietnamese *du chua* (pickled daikon, carrot and onion) and the best bread on the East Coast. "When we ran the bakery in Bangor, we used to serve Bahn Mi

sometimes," Brother Donald says. "One day, a customer came in with her tiny Vietnamese grandmother, and they ordered the sandwich. I asked her for her opinion, and she told me that while it was delicious, it was not quite correct. She then gifted me with her very own handwritten recipe for *du chua, and it's still* the recipe used to this day!"

Patrons are asked to put their cell phones away (house rules require that phones remain off), and enjoy the relaxed and amiable atmosphere. You won't want to miss the smiling comments from Brother Donald when he pops his head out of the kitchen. "How's the food?" he asks. Knowing mouths are too full to answer, he laughs, "I don't care. They told me to ask."

Truthfully, he does care. Brother Donald derives great pleasure from cooking and nurturing his guests, because, at the same time, he nurtures himself with his love of cooking, people, and a heaping serving of humor. Brother Donald tells a story of the best pea soup in the world. "Have you seen the sign that states The Friar's Brew House has the best pea soup in the world," he asks customers, adding, "You want to know how I know? I made the soup and I made the sign!"

Franciscan Friars, a religious order founded in 1209, take a vow of poverty, and because of this, proceeds from the brewery all go back to the operations of the brewery or to the monastery. Since part of the Friars' mission is to serve their community, it was important to the brothers that they created a community hub. "It's intimate," Brother Donald told *USA Today* upon opening the taproom. "It's the kind of place that you want to sit with friends and have a nice conversation and a beer."

"We're really in the right place at the right time," Brother Donald says. "In a very literal sense, it's a true godsend for the town of Bucksport."

————⊂•◆•⊃————

OPEN YEAR-ROUND
Tuesday thru Thursday, 11:30 a.m. to 4:00 p.m.
Friday and Saturday, 11:30 a.m. to 6:30 p.m.
207-702-9156

Nervous Nellie's Jams and Jellies

598 Sunshine Road
DEER ISLE

There are so many nooks and crannies to explore on Deer Isle. Take a hike through a boreal fog forest, walk to an island at low tide, or visit the local art galleries. Before you go, make sure to indulge in the magic and whimsy of Nervous Nellie's Jams and Jellies while you soak in the beauty of this island.

Upon arriving at Nervous Nellie's, your imagination takes flight. You came for the now-famous jams and jellies, but before you is a whimsical village complete with a jail, a wizard's tower, a fortune teller and a saloon. There are knights in the woods and a church in the distance. These are just a few of the life size sculptures that Peter Beerits has created.

A starving artist with a degree in sculpture from Southern California, Peter returned to Deer Isle, his childhood playground, in 1984 to find a way to sculpt and make a consistent living. With visions of whimsical bird sculptures and his mom's raspberry jelly recipe in hand, he started making and selling jars of the delicious jelly while collecting items from the local junk yard to integrate into his unique style of sculpture. Peter was an artist in the kitchen too, creating wonderful new recipes like Blue Razz Conserve, Sunshine Road Marmalade, and of course, recipes that include those delicious wild Maine blueberries. Each recipe was handcrafted in small batches to retain the vivid color, flavor and nutrients of each fruit.

After marrying Anne in 1996, Peter was able to concentrate solely on his sculptures while Anne managed the staff in the jelly kitchen. Using mostly Maine grown fruit, about 300 jars of jams, jellies or chutneys are lovingly hand-made each day in the tiny white cottage. Peek into the kitchen and smell the bubbling scent of Peter's mother's famous raspberry jelly. Then shop a bit in the adorable store with homegoods, Maine-made items, lots of jams and jellies, and copies of the Nervous Nellie Story. Now in its 10th and final chapter, Nervous Nellie, a whimsical bird born of Peter's imagination, is not only the name for the jam and jelly business, but the star of her own book series.

OPEN MAY TO OCTOBER
Tuesday thru Saturday, 11:00 a.m. to 5:00 p.m.
207-348-6182

SWEET CHEEKS BAKERY

70 US Highway One
VERONA ISLAND

Sometimes the most amazing places are hidden in plain sight. Over three million visitors must travel through the sweet little town of Bucksport to get to Acadia National Park each year. Most travelers choose to travel over the one-of-a-kind Penobscot Narrows Bridge, likely stopping to see the breathtaking views from the 420 foot tall observation tower. The bridge brings them onto the tiny Verona Island.

Halfway across the island is a nondescript building on the right; home to Sweet Cheeks Bakery. Watch for the sign with the smiling cherubic face on it, because Sweet Cheeks is worth a stop. Cases of exquisite cream puffs as big as your face, sticky rolls, donuts, apple fritters, fresh bread and gluten free cookies, cream horns and pies! It's a long way to Acadia, better stock up on some treats!

OPEN YEAR-ROUND
Wednesday, 9:00 a.m. to 5:00 pm
Thursday thru Saturday, 7:00 a.m. to 5:00 p.m.
Sunday, 8:00 a.m. to 3:00 p.m.
207-702-9363

Momo's Cheesecake

471 Main Street
ELLSWORTH

I n a world where crime and dishonesty regularly scroll across our newsfeeds, one baker believes in the goodness of people. Tucked away from the thriving city of Ellsworth lies an unassuming house next to a deep red garage, doors always unlocked, for the eager traveler that knows what lies within.

The first thing you might notice if you search for "Momo's Cheesecakes" online is their hours. Google says, "Open 24 hours." Facebook says, "Always open." That's because Momo's Cheesecakes never closes. With walls of commercial refrigerators filled to bursting with cheesecake slices in every imaginable flavor, customers just choose their favorites and leave their payment in the box before they leave. Momo's uses the honor system, so folks can serve themselves any time, day or night, and pay what they owe. With over sixty flavors to choose from, including strawberry rhubarb, lemon blueberry, pumpkin chocolate chip, and nutella, every cake is made from scratch. The sheer visual of this much rich delicious cheesecake is sure to have you drooling and digging around for utensils before you even get out of the driveway.

Brenda Ledezma started selling her cheesecakes while

bartending at the local Chinese food restaurant. Knowing that Brenda made a great cheesecake, friends would run into the restaurant and place their orders while Brenda worked. Seeing how much Brenda talked, her former boss, who owned the Chinese food restaurant where she worked for 22 years, started calling her Momo. Short for "motor mouth," the name stuck, and Momo hardly recognizes her birth name anymore.

Baking has always been a family affair. Sisters Momo and Nadine baked with their mom for all family functions like weddings, funerals, and parties. Momo's mother was an excellent cook and baker, and her father was all about the presentation. "He told us that if it doesn't look good, nobody will eat it, no matter how good it tastes," Momo says. "That's stuck with me."

Momo's cheesecakes soon became so popular that the disruption caused by friends stopping in to order cheesecake was affecting her work relationship at the restaurant. This was the moment the honor system was born. Momo had success leaving the completed cakes out in the garage and having customers leave the money in a cash box. Demand was growing and Momo told her husband that she'd like to expand on the idea, and decided to leave slices outside.

"Don't do that," her husband advised. "People will steal the slices."

"No they won't," Momo assured him. Through her love of baking and faith in humanity, Momo's Cheesecakes began.

Spending $300 to start the business in 2016, Momo got licensed for a home processors kitchen. Money was tight and Momo had no idea how she would afford the required sinks and ovens to run a home-based bakery. Loved by the community, gifts started to anonymously appear: a beautiful new

Viking oven, two hand sinks, and a two-bay sink. The community was so excited to help Momo so she could bake more, and that motivated Momo to build her business. At the beginning, the garage doors were left open so customers could help themselves, but after the first bear raided the garage (it was determined that the bear's favorite cheesecake flavor is peanut butter), the doors were closed at night, and customers were instructed to use the side door (and close it behind them).

Customers formed lines out the door to pick up their cheesecakes and drop off their cash or checks (Momo's now accepts Venmo as well). Soon the money flowed in and the cheesecakes went out. Momo still worked her day job for years, until finally leaving to work full-time at Momo's in 2020. She then hired her sister Nadine to help out. "The hardest part of the business was working full time," Momo says. "We actually got busier during the pandemic. I was afraid if I got sick, I'd lose the cheesecakes, and the cheesecakes are too important to me. I had worked my day job for twenty-two years, and they were good years, but it was time to move on in my life."

"I never imagined this could turn into a full-time job, with employees," Momo says. Employees include Momo's sister, her husband, and two nieces. Momo's biggest goal is to make enough so she can provide health insurance for the people who work for her. "Sure, sometimes I wish I had a bigger house, but it's more important that I help the people close to me."

Momo credits her sister with helping her run the business. "She's so book-smart," Momo says. "I couldn't do this without her." Her husband is an integral part of the business as well. Momo met her husband when they both worked at the Chinese restaurant. "It's been the best years of my life," she

says. "He supports me one-hundred percent."

Momo's bakes approximately one-hundred cheesecakes a day. Summer and fall are the busiest times, with business slowing down at the end of October. It picks up again for the holidays, and remains busy for the rest of the year. They start baking at around 7 am and continue for the next twelve hours, five days a week. They try to take Saturdays off, while Sundays are shorter days with only forty cheesecakes a day.

"What makes my cheesecakes so special is the love I put into them." Momo says. "I don't measure anything, but I do provide recipes for my other employees when they do some of the baking."

Momo's started making gluten-free products in 2021, since there was such a high demand for it. They try to accommodate their customers dietary needs, even trying a sugar-free cake, but it wasn't up to Momo's standards so she felt like she couldn't charge for it. They've learned that in order to keep their standards where they expect them, they can't make everybody happy. "We want to cater to everyone, but we just can't," Momo says. "We're glad there are other bakers who can offer sugar-free or vegan goodies."

"Our customers are amazing," Momo says. "They leave gifts for us; they sometimes leave extra money." Momo never

has to worry about waste because they always sell out. Wanting to contribute to the community that has been so good to her, Momo's donates ten percent of their proceeds to local non-profits and stuffs backpacks full of supplies every year when school is ready to re-open.

Look at the wall of sweet messages written on post-it notes from people all over the world. Everyone can agree that Momo's is a sweet story indeed.

━━━━━◁•◆•◁▷━━━━━

OPEN YEAR ROUND
24 hours
207-598-8772

PUGNUTS ICE CREAM

1276 Surry Road (Route 172)
SURRY

Homemade gelato and creamy ice cream in a dish, on a gluten free cone, or even as a freshly made cake!

OPEN SEASONALLY

Tuesday thru Thursday, 11:00 a.m. to 6:00 p.m.
Friday and Saturday, 11:00 a.m. to 8:00 p.m.
207-412-0086

Vasquez Mexican Takeout

38 Main Street
MILBRIDGE

Romana Vasquez started her business in 2000 in a bus, serving recipes learned from her childhood in central Mexico. Handmade flour tortillas stuffed and wrapped into delicious burritos, chimichangas hot out of the fryer, and beans, boiled for hours, to be mashed into the refried beans served on the side. For 13 years, Romana served migrant workers laboring in the wild blueberry fields. She loved to cook and found great fulfillment in the corn and flour doughs that she would transform into the spicy delicacies of her youth.

Always dreaming of expanding and not wanting to move from place to place with the bus, Romana and her husband purchased the house at 38 Main Street in Milbridge in 2014. They fixed up their new home and installed a space for Romana's Dream, Vasquez Mexican Takeout.

Over 20 years have passed since Romana started creating in Maine. Her family has grown; 24 members of the family pitch in at the restaurant through the summer. Her daughters, son, grandchildren, and even a great grandchild help Romana and her husband make tortillas, salsa, fill the sour cream, and provide that authentic Mexican experience that they are famous for.

"Everything is made from scratch," daughter Juliana says. "It may take a while to get your food as we make everything from scratch. We are making the taco from the fresh tortilla dough as soon as you order." You won't find any packaged taco shells at Vasquez's.

In order to provide a gluten free option, about 150 flour tortillas are made before the restaurant opens. Then, everything is cleaned and sanitized, with separate fryers used to prevent cross contamination. When asked how many corn tortillas get made each day, Juliana laughs, "I don't know! Alot!" The most popular dishes are chimichangas and tacos. Their nachos are piled high with meat, cheese, lettuce and tomato and the tamales are exceptional.

Romana Vasquez offers a special treat for the children of her community. "Free hot chocolate, strawberry and chocolate conchas (a Mexican sweet bread also called pan dulce) and tamales are given to all of the neighborhood children on Halloween," Juliana says. "It is my mother's passion to cook and share her food."

Vasquez Mexican Takeout is only open April through October. However, if you were to drive by after school any day, you would see the children of the family gathering at Romana's. Her daughter says, "She just loves to cook for everyone."

OPEN SEASONALLY MONDAY THRU FRIDAY
10:00 a.m. to 7:00 p.m.
207-546-2219

M & L Seafood

638 Beach Rd
LINCOLNVILLE

Fresh, steamed lobstah! A roadside stand located in the home of owners Mike and Lynn, locals and tourists can grab a steamed lobster, uncooked crab meat, scallops, and steamers right off the boat. It doesn't get any fresher than this unless you catch it yourself!

OPEN DAILY
11:00 a.m. to 6:00 p.m.
207-763-3983

Dolce Vita Farm & Bakery

488 Beach Rd,
LINCOLNVILLE

ose Lowell's life changed in a split second. In 1999, she had just graduated from the Downeast School of Massage. With a thriving massage practice, Rose was on her way to success. A drunk driver would change her path.

After a debilitating accident that left her trapped in a car for hours, Rose spent months in a wheelchair, and followed with two years in physical therapy and rehab. During her recovery, Rose spent a lot of time reflecting on her life. The things she thought were important before her accident no longer seemed so important. "Things become clearer when you think you're going to die," Rose says.

That clarity allowed Rose to realize that the extensive injuries to her shoulder and foot meant she would not be able to continue as a massage therapist. "I was so proud of myself for graduating and starting a business," Rose says. "But I knew I had to let it go."

Her team of doctors told her that getting her life back would be a long journey, and Rose traveled back and forth to Portland for medical treatment during her recovery. "Barnes & Noble became the highlights of those trips," Rose says. Armed with books on healing and self-discovery, Rose was on a path to find her new purpose. She read, she researched, and she even created a vision board of what she wanted for her life. What she found astonished her.

"Almost everything on my vision board—music, food, linens, colors, villas, was from Tuscany," Rose remembers. Rose had never actually been to Italy. She never even thought about going to Italy. "I didn't like to fly," Rose says, "but Italy kept coming up for me, over and over again."

The thoughts of Tuscany wouldn't leave her head. She felt herself compelled to read books on the area, watch movies, and learn all that she could. Soon, she knew she had to visit. But with her injuries, she wasn't sure she'd be able to travel anywhere, let alone overseas."I talked to my surgeon about it," Rose remembers. "He thought that if I worked hard in physical therapy, I might be able to do it eventually, and suggested I check in a month later." Rose did just that, and in another four weeks, she was cleared by her doctor to travel. The only stipulation was that she stop at L.L. Bean and buy a special pair of orthotic boots, which she did immediately.

Since the Internet wasn't as accessible as it is today, Rose contacted a travel agent. As soon as the agent heard Rose speak about Tuscany, she knew right where to send her. "I hadn't traveled that far alone before," Rose says. "I had to use a cane to walk. I was scared to death."

It turns out the travel agent sent her to Castello di Spannocchia, an 1100-acre estate that includes a working organic farm, an education center, and a multinational community. "I truly felt like Dorothy in The Wizard of Oz," Rose says, her eyes lighting up at the memory. "It was the most amazing,

magical place I'd ever been. It was just like the movies I'd seen, with mountains, valleys, and people chattering in Italian in the courtyard. I knew I'd found my special place."

While there was a lot to love at Spannocchia, Rose gravitated toward the kitchen. She befriended the estate's chef and baker, who has since visited Maine to see her several times. She learned how to make authentic Italian dishes while she was there, and she learned the Italian customs around food. When it was time to go home, the only thing she could think about was when she would get the chance to go back.

Since that first visit, Rose has traveled to Italy 27 times in 22 years. She worked on an organic farm for months at a time, she worked in Italian kitchens, and she even brought groups there for food and wine tours. She immersed herself in the language, the cuisine, and the culture.

Each and every time she returned to Maine, she was more inspired. Seven years after she started traveling to Italy, she decided to buy a wood oven so she could make authentic Italian breads and pizzas. She named the oven "Arabella," which means "answered prayer." "The first time I made a fire in that oven, I cried," Rose says. "I made about ten pizzas that first night. I think I was the happiest person on Earth."

Rose grows her own vegetables and uses them whenever she can. Naming her farm Dolce Vita, which means "sweet life," Rose uses her own tomatoes for her sauce, and sources locally for meats. Her best-selling pizzas include a local shitake pizza, and, believe it or not, a red grape pizza (she got the idea for this one in Italy), featuring grapes, fennel, sausage, blue cheese, and red onions. "It takes two hours to make a batch of pizza dough and one hour to cook the sauce," Rose says. When she has time, she makes her own lasagna noodles. "Using homemade pasta is truly special," Rose says.

For breakfast, she bakes scones, brioche do chocolate, almond marzipan, Italian crustadas with apricot or fig and ginger jam inside, and a special "oatmeal everything" cookie. Desserts include cannolis, tiramisu, chocolate cake, and cookies. Her favorite bread to bake is sourdough, and all of this is lovingly created with her trusty oven, Arabella. "I'm so lucky. I have this beautiful oven," Rose says. "She is my biggest and greatest teacher. I am humbled every time I work with her."

Her daughter Melissa has been working with her at Dolce Vita lately, and Rose is happy for the help. "Even all of these years after the accident, I still don't have range of motion in my shoulder," Rose says. Arthritis has set in her feet, and her doctors are recommending another surgery. "I love cooking and I get so much joy from feeding folks," Rose says. "But I'm getting older. I'd like to retire someday, cook for my family and friends, and host dinner parties. No matter how old I get, I'll always host Sunday night dinner for the people I care about."

But she's not ready to retire yet! Rose hopes to be able

to provide food for her community for years to come. "I love to cook for people. I have been given the opportunity to be my own boss, and I'm so grateful for the community of Lincolnville. The people here are caring, loving and supportive."

Rose is grateful when she reflects on the accident that changed her life, brought her to Italy, and created a way for her to provide for her community. "Life is about choices," Rose says. "I could have given up. We all have the ability to take the best from every situation. Life gave me lemons and I made lemonade... or rather, limoncello!"

⊂◦◆◦⊃

PIZZA OPEN LATE APRIL TO OCTOBER, FRIDAY EVENINGS
Bakehouse open Saturdays, 9:00 a.m. to 2:00 p.m.
207-323-1052

Rose Cottage Bakery

36 Limerock Street
CAMDEN

Past downtown Camden, away from the hubbub of traffic, lies one of the area's best kept secrets. A tiny cottage on Limerock Street, home to *Down East* magazine's Best Bakery of 2017, a line winds down the street and around the corner. At the front of that line is Megan. "Welcome to Rose Cottage Bakery! Who would like to help in the bakery today?" Megan (pronounced Mee-gan) Murphy greets her customers each Saturday morning in a cute, floral apron. While the lines often extend out to the street, she welcomes each and every person and tells them what she is offering that day. "At the beginning, customers would write the menu on the sandwich board for me. They put together their own boxes, and they even helped behind the counter," Megan says. "It's now become a tradition that two customers help me open the French doors leading to the bakery when we open in the morning." People raise their hands high in hopes of being chosen to work alongside Megan for a few hours. Volunteers are chosen and patrons patiently wait for their turn inside to choose their sweet treats. Neighbors enjoy conversation and new friends are made with those from away that were lucky enough to know about the sweet little bakery that quietly resides in Megan's quaint home.

Megan has a sweet tooth. While raising her children on Cliff Island in Casco Bay, she realized there was no place to buy baked goods, so she taught herself to make them. Proud to be self-trained, Megan ran a tiny bakery on Islesboro, where they sold out nearly every day. She realized she had found success when she met a well-to-do couple at a stand at the local farmer's market. The couple was planning their wedding, and since it was going to be an afternoon wedding, they were searching for a unique cake. The husband-to-be purchased one of Megan's cinnamon rolls, because his wife had never had one before. After just one bite, the couple pleaded with Megan to create the rolls for their wedding in lieu of a wedding cake. Excited for the challenge, Megan agreed. At that time, she only had one oven, but she knew she wanted the goodies to be fresh. Some suggested she freeze the dough in advance, but she refused. "If my name is going to be on it, it has to be fresh."

On the day of the wedding, Megan recruited four of her neighbors, asking them to pre-heat their ovens to 350 degrees, and brought the uncooked rolls to their homes. It was pouring that day, so, dressed in rain gear, Megan sprinted back and forth between their houses to check on them. When the pastries were ready, Megan drove a van borrowed from the local yacht yard and loaded up trays of cinnamon buns. She chauffeured them to the wedding venue, backed the truck up to the

tent, and arranged the still-warm buns on the dessert table. The wedding guests loved them, and when she came back later to pick up the trays, every cinnamon bun had been eaten.

When Megan moved from Islesboro to the mainland, she found a property in Camden with both a house and a garage, where she sells her delicious baked treats. Filled with whimsical touches like re-purposed French doors that greet customers each morning, a thrift-store jewelry case transformed into a baker's case, a pink and white Karavan trailer, and even a shed that was brought to Camden on a barge from her former property on Islesboro, Rose Cottage Bakery is as delightful as it is delicious. Customers often stroll through her backyard, finding a cozy spot to have tea or enjoy a freshly baked muffin, creating a magical experience right on her property.

The summer season is filled with tourists, and Megan sometimes gets stressed that those at the end of the line won't get what they came for. "We usually sell out by 11 am," she says. "I feel terrible when we sell out before everyone has been served." But still, Megan refuses to compromise on quality. "I get up extra early so I can bake more. My customers expect the highest quality, and that means everything is made fresh."

Cinnamon rolls still remain a staple and one of Rose Cottage Bakery's most popular items. Other treats on the menu include banana walnut crumb muffins, chocolate peanut butter chip cookies topped with a dark chocolate peanut butter ganache, Nutella stuffed brownies, and summer peach muffins with ginger streusel. Savory scones such as spinach, feta, and pine nuts or bacon, cheddar, and chives are also often on the menu alongside Megans famous Rose Cottage Cakes.

While zoning restrictions in a residential neighborhood means Rose Cottage Bakery can only be open during limited hours, a home-based bakery allows Megan to fulfill her dream while still being present for her children. "I've always worked at very small bakeries, elbow-to-elbow with others," she says.

"I was trained to work in tiny places and have always brought my children along." Megan's oldest son grew up in the storage room of a bakery in New Hampshire, where he would color, play, and even help his mom collect lemon balm from the gardens outside. "Back then, there were no gadgets," Megan said, "so my kids did a lot of baking and assisting. All of them are now excellent in the kitchen."

Megan knows how important her community is. From the customers who first open the doors in the morning to the volunteers who help her behind the counter on her busiest days, she tries to make each one a priority. "I'm grateful for the regulars who know me well enough to pronounce my name correctly," she says. "And I'm grateful for the summer people who stand in line waiting for what they call 'the best cinnamon rolls in the world.'"

<hr>

OPEN SEASONALLY
Saturday mornings only and by special order
207-323-5793

Street Food 330

330 Commercial Street
ROCKPORT

Serving up multicultural vegetarian and pescatarian plant-based food to Mid-coast Maine, Street Food 330 blends two cultural cuisines: Cambodia and the American Southwest.

Proprietors Stephanie Jeanne Turner and Marykate Moriarty met when Stephanie was working as a stylist at Salon Suites by the Sea, a salon she owns with her husband, Jim. Marykate was in the next chair and overheard Stephanie speaking of the Asian market she frequents. Bonding over Asian cuisine, the two women realized that they had a lot in common.

After hearing stories of Cambodia from her husband who was a Marine during the Vietnam War, Stephanie visited Cambodia and fell in love with the country and the people. Meanwhile, Marykate spent 20 of her 31 years of her life in Cambodia. Her father, also stationed in Cambodia when he was a Marine in the Vietnam War, took his wife and children from New England to Cambodia, where they spent years doing mission work and building schools.

Marykate had studied the cuisine and spent many hours cooking Cambodian dishes while dreaming of having a small restaurant of her own one day. After divorcing her husband, a Cambodian Prince, she and her daughter arrived in Maine where Marykate eventually purchased a food cart that she set up at a local brewery not long before she met Stephanie.

Stephanie and her husband had just opened Salon Suites in Rockport, but Stephanie had always dreamed of having a restaurant that served delicious authentic burritos. Reliving the food of Cambodia through discussion with Marykate got Stephanie thinking. The two women realized that with their combined passion and Marykate's culinary experience, their dreams of having a restaurant could come true.

Stephanie asked her landlord if she could also rent the pergola that was next to Salon Suites. He agreed to let her enclose the space and open the small takeout restaurant. "I could not have done this without my husband," Stephanie says. "Rockport does not allow take-out or food trucks. So, Jim had to be super creative." To be considered a restaurant, they needed a bathroom in the tiny 20 x 20 space. Stephanie certainly did not want the bathroom door opening into her kitchen, so Jim found a way to convert a 5 x 7 space into a bathroom, with the door leading in from outside. This satisfied the town, and they were able to get licensed as a restaurant.

Ecstatic, Stephanie combines mangoes, limes, cilantro, peppers, tamarin, black beans and garacho beans cooked for over 4 hours, to make authentic burritos with lime cilantro. She especially loves foods that are simple in their presentation, like Mexican slaw, salsa, pickled onion and creama. "Who doesn't like quesadillas," Stephanie asks with a smile. "They can be simple, as in a small plain cheese for kids, but more complex for those of us with more adventurous tasetbuds as we journey along."

Meanwhile, Marykate prepares all of the Asian/ Khmer cooking like fresh spring rolls, shredded green Vietnamese salad, Bahn Hoi noodle bowls with garlic cilantro shrimp or tofu, and lime rice. "Marykate's lime rice is one of my staples," enthuses Stephanie.

The partnership of these women and these cuisines will bring in customers looking for local produce, healthy options, and mouth-watering meals to-go.

———◦•◆•◦———

Wednesday thru Saturday, 11:00 a.m to 6:00 p.m.
207-706-4989

Namaste Indian Food

930 Commercial Street
ROCKPORT

There were a few encounters that caused Deepa Patel (Dee) and her sister-in-law Krishna Patel to open Namaste Indian Food after moving to Rockport to run the motel Ledges By The Bay. "A woman randomly stopped me in Walmart one day," Dee says, "and asked me if I sold Indian food. When I said I didn't, she brought me to the spice aisle so I could help her pick out the right spices to make her own." These experiences continued to happen. "I used to work in a doctor's office," Dee says. "Sometimes I brought my food into the office to share with my co-workers. They loved it, and recommended that I start selling it."

But the real impetus for Namaste Indian Food happened on the breakwater in Rockland. Dee and Krishna were taking a walk when a woman approached them. "Do you cook Indian food?" she asked. "Or do you sell it?" At this time, they didn't sell their food, but Dee and Krishna chatted with the woman. It turns out she was a social worker, just like Krishna, and she was a huge fan of Indian food. The more they spoke, the more interesting the idea of opening a restaurant became.

Dee seriously considered this. There are not many Indian food restaurants in Midcoast Maine. The closest places can be found in Brunswick, the Augusta area, the Bangor area, and Bar Harbor, but all of those towns are well over an hour's drive from the Camden-Rockport area.

"There seemed to be a real desire for Indian food," Dee says.

Dee, who grew up in India, moved to the United States in 2008. She spent five years in New Jersey, then followed her husband to Augusta for a job opportunity. When they settled in the Midcoast to open The Ledges By The Bay, Dee's mom, who had been in India, followed. Her in-laws were already here, so she had a supportive family nearby. Krishna came to the United States in 2001, and currently divides her time between New Jersey and Maine.

While Dee and Krishna, with their families, knew how to run a motel, they had no experience in starting a restaurant. "We had no idea where to begin," Krishna says, "but we wanted to try."

They knew one thing. Dee would be the head chef. Dee learned to cook while growing up in Gujarat, India, where most of the people are vegetarian and food is a central part of life. "Back in those days, as women, we grew up in the kitchen next to our moms and grandmothers," Dee says. "I was always interested in cooking and trying new recipes." When she was a young teenager, she would clip the weekly recipes from the newspaper. She'd try them out, tweaking them to make them her own. "I was passionate about trying new recipes," Dee remembers. "As I did, I became more confident with ingredients, spices, and how to combine those."

"Not only is Dee a passionate cook," Krishna says. "But she truly loves to feed people." Dee believes in using only fresh ingredients in all of her made-from-scratch recipes. "When you prepare food with purpose and caring, those intentions come through in the flavor," Dee says.

Dee's mother and mother in law help with cooking, and the rest of her family helps in the restaurant. Krishna even comes up from New Jersey on the weekends to assist. "I have huge family support," Dee says. "Without my family, it would be almost impossible to do anything."

They also have huge community support, which was a pleasant surprise. "We were worried when we first started," Dee says. "We were not professional cooks. I learned from watching my grandmother and my mother since childhood."

In order to help calm their fears, Namaste Indian Food, which opened in June of 2019, started small. "We decided to have limited offerings, take-out only, and see how the community responded," Krishna says.

Dee remembers being nervous at the beginning. "What if they don't like my food," Dee laughs. "But that didn't happen. They liked it!"

That's an understatement. The community loved her food. "There is so much community support here," Dee says. "Being different sometimes, we weren't sure how people would respond. But we were really welcomed here in the Mid-coast. Our community makes us feel at home."

Krishna agrees. "We don't have words for how welcome we feel."

Most people in the area Dee is from in India are vegetarian. "We wanted to do something that not only we enjoy, but something the community would enjoy, too," Dee says. "We were worried at first that we don't offer meat, but people appreciate the vegetarian food. They tell us they don't miss the meat at all."

Each region of India speaks a different language, wears different clothes, and eats different foods. "Indian cuisine is divided into two regions," Dee says. "The food in the North consists of curries, naan, rice, and daal, while the South focuses on things like dosas and sambar." While Dee's hometown is in the middle of India, Namaste focuses more on

Northern recipes. "We have tried some South Indian dishes as specials," Dee says, "but most folks in the mid-coast are more familiar with the Northern recipes, so we mostly make those. We'll make South Indian recipe specials so people can have that experience."

"In India, North Indian people eat certain foods because of their weather, which is cooler," Krishna says. "South India has more tropical foods. Since our customers here in Maine are in a northern climate, we should eat more in line with that climate. Each of the spices help our health, and especially our digestive system. Indian food is not only food, but it's also healthy!"

Rather than serve different items every weekend, like they did when they first opened, Namaste has created an established menu. "We constantly asked our customers what they liked, and that's how we learned what people wanted," Dee says. "Feedback, feedback, feedback!" They offer specials, however, and those will get added to the menu with enough customer support.

Dee still experiments with new recipes and has recently developed a new customer favorite: banana curry. "It was started as a special item but has become a permanent menu item because people love it," Dee says. "I didn't know it would be so popular!"

Other customer favorites include the paneer dishes such as palak paneer, Indian fried cheese cooked with spinach, cream, and spices and paneer tikka masala, Indian fried cheese cooked with tomatoes, cream, spices, and cashews. Plenty of vegan dishes, such as eggplant curry and chana masala, can also be found on the menu. Gluten-free and nut-free options are available as well.

Since Dee and Krishna still have small children at home, they will continue to keep Namaste Indian food relatively small and only open on weekends. "We hope to balance our family life and our business life," Dee says.

Diners are welcome to take-out or eat-in. The food can be picked up at the front desk of Ledges by the Sea, where customers can eat in the dining room featuring a wall of windows that offers spectacular views of the Penobscot Bay. There is also a deck and picnic tables on the back lawn for those who would like to enjoy those same views outdoors.

Locals make up the majority of Namaste's customer base,

but travelers come too, especially the folks who stay at the
Ledges during the summer months. "We bring their food right
to their rooms," Krishna says. "When they check in and they
smell the food, they decide to order right then and there!"

"We love that most of our customers are locals," Dee says.
"We truly love being a part of this warm and welcoming community, and we're grateful that we can offer something that
makes them happy in return."

━━━◇•◆•◇━━━

OPEN YEAR ROUND
Friday thru Sunday, 11:00 a.m. to 8:00 p.m.
207-992-6347

Thai Tugboat

Rockland Ferry Terminal
ROCKLAND

I n a mere 12 x 16 space in the parking lot of the Rockland
ferry terminal, Thai Tugboat's traditional dishes are lovingly
made by two people who discovered each other over these very
meals.

Sulaleewal Palakawong, affectionately known as Sue,
opened Thai Tugboat in the summer of 2011. Born in Bang-
kok, Thailand and raised in China, she learned to cook from
watching her mother prepare traditional Thai dishes like
curry, pad thai, and peanut sauce. Sue came to the United
States in 2004, after seeing a movie about snow. "I wanted to
touch it!" she says with a hearty laugh.

Sue had plenty of opportunity to play in the snow while
working at Thai restaurants in Boston, Camden, and Rockland. She dreamed of opening her own business, but with rents
high, she had a hard time finding something affordable. Sue
was thrilled when the opportunity to open Thai Tugboat in its
current location—a seasonal building—came up.

Sue's partner Dan Greene is a lifelong Mainer who just
happened to like Thai food. He and Sue met the first season
Thai Tugboat opened when Dan would come for lunch during

his work breaks. The pair hit it off, and Dan has been by Sue's side ever since. "It was a new adventure for me," says Dan. "I never worked in the restaurant business before, but I learned how to cook, use the fryer, prep vegetables and with Sue's help, I even learned how to make sauces."

Overlooking the Rockland harbor, Thai Tugboat's menu includes appetizers such as delicate steamed dumplings filled with sweet shrimp and dipped in a ginger soy sauce, as well as tiny crunchy samosas stuffed with potato, carrot, and cilantro dipped in a Thai chili sauce. Entree options include a Thai green curry made with coconut milk and curry paste over freshly steamed broccoli, green beans, and carrots, and chicken pad thai, which features a generous portion of chicken mingled with egg noodles and a crunchy carrot and cabbage garnish. Dan and Sue buy their vegetables fresh every day, and the authentic peanut sauce is a Thai specialty. Sue is most excited about the Jasmine rice from Thailand that she orders in bulk so her dishes taste just like the recipes her mom used to make.

For those who prefer more typical Maine faire, Thai Tugboat also offers fried haddock, shrimp, scallops, and clams. There is no indoor seating, but picnic-style tables are available for outdoor seating. Takeout is also available.

Although the restaurant gets quite a bit of tourists via ferry traffic, they've built up their local following over the years, and they're grateful for those folks who keep coming back. In the off-season, Sue relaxes and takes it easy. "The restaurant business is hard work," Dan says. "She works all day long non-stop and deserves a break." Sue will occasionally teach cooking classes, while Dan works in the food department

at the Maine General Hospital in Augusta. "They're good enough to hold the job for me, so I can go back in the fall through the spring," Dan adds.

"We love to make good Thai food," Sue says. "I'm happy I can bring these flavors from my home country to Maine."

<hr/>

OPEN MAY THROUGH LABOR DAY
Wednesday thru Monday, 11:00 a.m. to 5:00 p.m.

Mé Lon Togo

10 Leland Street
ROCKLAND

While Rockland is a pretty popular food town and not exactly "out of the way," this West African bistro started in an old tavern off Route 1 in Searsport. From there, they moved to Camden, and most recently, they've found their home in Rockland.

According to Mé Lon Togo's website, Chef-owner Jordan Benissan is from Togo, a small country on the Gulf of Guinea. A master polyrhythmic drummer, Jordan came to Maine in the 1990s to teach West African music and music theory at Colby College. Missing home and craving community, he began experimenting in the kitchen with the hope of recreating the nostalgic flavors of Togo to share with his community in Maine.

He started hosting dinner parties and quickly became a local celebrity. As word spread of his incredible West African feasts—which often included live music and flowing cocktails—he decided to open his own restaurant. With the encouragement of his community and support from friends and family, he was very quickly able to make a name for himself in the culinary world.

At Mé Lon Togo (which translates to "I love Togo"), Jordan Benissan welcomes you to a warm, casual dining room filled with the aromas of his childhood. Jordan pulls from West Africa's indigenous and colonial influences to establish his unique representation of West African cuisine in Maine. It is not uncommon for Jordan to pull up a chair at your table or grab a drum and play a brief set for his guests. Mé Lon Togo is a dinner party with world class cocktails, sophisticated cuisine, and a dedicated host.

Benissan started cooking because he wanted to recreate dishes from his childhood. "I realized that I really missed food from home," he told *Down East* magazine. "I tried to cook what I'd learned from my mother, and after a while, I started to think wow, this really tastes good."

The menu includes dishes like Mé Lon Togo stew, a savory stew made with sweet potato, plantain, eggplant, zucchini, portobello and shiitake mushrooms, celery, chickpeas, and cooked in a West African blend of herbs and spices.

Benissan's vision has been "to have a place where people feel like they are at home," he told Central Maine reporters. "I want them to have the comfort of home and a relaxed atmosphere to enjoy a fine dining experience and also enjoy the finest cuisine from Togo, West Africa and Europe."

Open Thursday thru Sunday, 5:00 to 9:00 p.m.
207-872-9146

Laurel's Dolce Vita Italian Bakery

350 Main Street
THOMASTON

2 3-year-old Laurel Christopher, a fourth generation Italian, grew up in the kitchen with her mom. She now lives above her shop and says, "Nothing beats the feeling of waking up and going downstairs to bake for a few hours."

Laurels favorite thing to make is Napoleans. When she was younger, the delicate puff pastry layered with clouds of creamy delicious vanilla pastry cream was her mom's favorite treat. Laurel learned how to make them and they are now her best-selling item in the bakery.

When asked what her secret to success is, she answers, "Everything is made from scratch. Baked fresh each day from small batches for that one-of-a-kind taste." She says that she and her mom are pretty relaxed, and just want to see you come in with a smile on your face and leave happier than when you came in.

Laurel's menu changes every single day, but, Laurel says, "Anything you have ever seen on previous menus, including freshly made pasta, can be special ordered. Just ask!"

———◦•◆•◦———

Open Tuesday thru Sunday
9:00 a.m. to 2:00 p.m. or when sold out
207-354-5242

ANCHO HONEY

6 Wallston Road
TENANTS HARBOR

Offering an eat-in option, an outdoor dining option, or take-out, Ancho Honey sells a variety of gourmet grilled cheese sandwiches, with drool-worthy names like The Brie and Blue (warm brie cheese, bacon, and blueberry preserves), The Brisket Twister (braised brisket, havarti cheese, caramelized onions, and horseradish aioli), and The Satay All Day (havarti cheese, smoked chicken breast, housemade peanut satay sauce, jalapenos, cilantro slaw, and chopped peanuts).

Customers can also pick food up from their grab-and-go cases (which usually includes creative kinds of mac and cheese and salads) or from their freezer (where you'll find items like shredded pork shoulder verde rigatoni or lentils with andouille sausage and fresh spinach).

Open Wednesday thru Sunday
11:00 a.m. to 7:00 p.m.
207-372-2111

Raegamuffins

1552 State Street
VEAZIE

As a celiac patient, Rachel Lane found herself constantly experimenting with recipes to convert them to gluten free. She hoped to one day open a bakery that caters to folks like herself, and, after attending culinary school at The New England Culinary Institute followed by an internship at a Boston bakery, Rachel (called Rae by her family, hence the spelling of her shop), opened Raegamuffins GF Bakery in 2014 at just 22 years old.

In addition to being completely gluten-free, Raegamuffins is also a peanut and tree-nut free facility. "In our pursuit to be as inclusive as possible, we carefully screen our ingredients to ensure no peanut or tree-nut exposure," Rachel says. The bakery also makes some dairy-free and vegan goodies, and even sugar-free items by request.

Along with a wide array of traditional doughnuts, muffins, cakes, breads, and cookies, Raegamuffins Bakery also features mouth-watering creations like cake batter doughnuts, coconut caramel muffins, and vegan pumpkin chocolate chip whoopie pies. Even with all of those creative concoctions, Raegamuffins is known for their Amazeballs, a delicious concoction of cake and ganache that closely resembles a truffle. "This treat was actually a genius idea born of a muffin mistake," Rachel says. "Overfilled pans caused the muffin tops to break off. Not wanting to waste them, I mixed the muffin with a vegan ganache and coconut to create the Amazeball!" Raegamuffins now features a huge selection of Amazeballs like lemon, birthday cake, and spice cake. Cakes can be intricately designed and customized for any occasion, and all of Rachel's baked goods look just as luscious as they taste.

For folks with a more savory palette, Rachel also creates lasagnas, pot pies, shepherd's pies, and pizza crusts, and keeps her freezer stocked with them for customers to take home.

Up in the wee hours and on your feet all day, a baker's job

is difficult. Rachel has an additional challenge to contend with. Diagnosed with Postural Orthostateic Tachycardis Syndrome (POTS), Rachel has to be careful about being on her feet too long or transitioning too quickly from sitting to standing. Doing so may cause her heart rate to spike, which can result in fainting spells. But running Raegamuffin's is a job born of passion, so Rachel uses her love of her craft and pure determination to solve this issue. With a counter height chair on rollers, you will see Rachel zip around her shop doing what she loves most.

✦

OPEN YEAR ROUND
Gluten-free, nut-free, vegan options.
Wednesday thru Saturday, 6:30 a.m. to 2:00 p.m.
207-942-9400

Yum Bake Shop

215 Penobscot Ave Unit B
MILLINOCKET

John and Maria Rowe met in Clearwater, Florida; Maria cleaned at the restaurant where John was a cook. Maria had a ten-year visa from Poland and had been in the U.S. for just a year. "I helped Maria clean from midnight to 4 a.m.," John says, "since that was the only way for us to spend time together."

Looking for a new beginning together, John and Maria left Florida for Maine in 2002 when John accepted a job as first mate on a Whale Watch out of Boothbay Harbor. No stranger to hard work, Maria worked at multiple Bed and Breakfasts to help make ends meet.

Multi-talented and industrious, John later started selling baked goods at the flea market in Searsport where he met Paul Naron, founder of The United Farmer's Market of Maine. John helped Paul open the indoor farmers market in 2017, where he had a booth up until 2021. John and Maria were well known faces at The United Farmers Market of Maine, selling meals like pulled pork, quiche, meatballs, Italian sausages, soups, sandwiches, and their incredibly popular desserts.

A self-professed "old hippie," John used to camp at Katahdin and the surrounding lakes when he was younger, and Maria enjoys the quiet atmosphere of Northern Maine. With these thoughts in mind, they realized that there was nowhere in Millinocket to eat that provided a full menu of baked goods and home-cooked meals. John and Maria knew this was the perfect opportunity to enjoy the quiet beauty of Northern Maine while introducing an entirely new clientele to their homemade food, so, they decided to open a shop.

"There are a lot of retired mill workers in the area," John says, "and we provide hearty, homestyle meals at a reasonable price." An enthusiastic Maria adds, "There's no other bakery for miles around and the locals are just delighted that we are here. We're delighted to be here!"

OPEN YEAR ROUND
Thursday, Friday, Saturday, 9:00 a.m. to 5:00 p.m.
207-447-9746

Peace, Love, & Waffles

1282 Bangor Road
Dover-Foxcroft

Erin Riley, the founder of Peace, Love, & Waffles considers herself a hippie. Born in the 1960s, Erin loves all things from the era of peace and love: the decor, the music, but especially the attitude. "My mom really wanted to open a restaurant where people would feel loved and welcomed," says Michael Begley, Erin's son and General Manager-turned-owner.

Michael, who bought the restaurant from his mom so she could retire and take care of her family members who have health-related problems, can't take credit for the idea of Peace, Love, Waffles. That was all his mom's idea. While living in Colorado, she dreamed of starting an electric food truck that only made waffles. They opted for a restaurant rather than a food truck, but they do have an all-electric kitchen.

While Erin was dreaming of a waffle restaurant, Michael was teaching English in Korea. Upon returning to the states, he helped a friend run his food truck, and in the summer of 2019, his mom called him with the idea of Peace, Love, & Waffles. Michael, who was born and raised in Kansas and went to school in Colorado, decided to follow his mom to Maine to help her pursue her dream. "I definitely think of Maine as my home

now. It's such a blessing that I ended up here, and I hope to grow with the business."

Although Michael is new to Maine, he realizes how special it is. "We're so lucky to have amazing products right here in the state and using as many local goods as we can is important to us," Michael says. "Some items are so local they come from our backyard! We have fresh blueberries, blackberries, pear trees, and apple trees on our property." Many summer and fall specials include their own fruit, so the customer knows they're getting a quality, authentic product. The restaurant uses maple syrup from Bob's Sugarhouse in Dover-Foxcroft and G&M maple syrup in Charleston, with flavors like cinnamon infused maple syrup, habanero maple syrup, and bourbon barrel-aged syrup, that are available to enjoy in the restaurant or to purchase. All of their breakfast meats go through Herring Brothers Butcher Shop in Guilford, about ten miles north of the restaurant, and they use the produce from Stutzman's Farm in Sangerville.

The restaurant, which opened in November of 2019, had to shut down five months later due to the Covid pandemic. Luckily, Peace, Love, & Waffles built up quite a following, so they were ready to wait it out. They decided to go one step further. They found a new location for Peace, Love, & Waffles, an 1800s-era barn that they renovated into a restaurant.

The new location brought in people from farther away than the immediate area. "People would talk about this really cool waffle place that opened up," Michael says. "They loved the food and the atmosphere, which has this hippy chic, happy vibe." Pictures of laugh-out-loud quotes like, "Coffee: Because you never got a pony" and "Decaf only works if you throw it at people" adorn the walls, along with inspirational quotes like

"When the power of love overcomes a love of power, the world will know" and "Peace is not something you wish for. It's something you make, something you do, something you are, and something you give away."

The natural beauty of the restaurant doesn't go unnoticed. Using talents his mom learned from a former career as an interior designer, the restaurant's hippy chic decor complements the refreshed barn. Outdoor seating is available when weather permits. "We have a real park-like setting that we've created behind the barn," Michael says. "We try to keep our outdoor seating open as long as possible."

Mainers drive for hours to sample some waffles, and that motivates Michael to be sure that they enjoy every bite. "It's so important that folks enjoy their meal, their time, and that they think it's worth the drive. When we have people traveling those distances, we don't want to disappoint."

With over twenty-one different flavors on the menu, folks are sure to find a favorite. Along with classics like the "All-American," a waffle with two eggs and your choice of ham, bacon, or sausage or the "Strawberry" waffle, a Belgian waffle infused with strawberry puree, homemade whipped cream cheese, and strawberries on top, there are also unique creations like the "Tree Hugger," a Belgian waffle loaded with Greek yogurt, granola, nuts, and three kinds of berries and the "Java," an espresso-infused waffle with homemade whipped creamed cheese, mocha sauce, and topped with chocolate covered espresso beans. Gluten-free, vegan, and vegetarian waffles are also available. "One of our best-selling vegetarian waffles is a creamy polenta waffle with sun-dried tomatoes and parmesan cheese inside, and that goes right into the batter that goes into the waffle iron," Michael says. "Then we add a rich, garlic cheese sauce to go on top."

Lake lovers bring folks in over the summer, and leaf-peepers bring them in over the fall season. They even get snowmobilers in the winter, but locals, who typically stay away during the busy seasons of summer and fall, make up most of the customer base for the rest of the year. "I love that locals bring their family and friends who are visiting here," Michael says. "As much as I care for this place, it seems that locals also take pride in this little breakfast spot that they get to call their own."

With no marketing budget, Peace, Love, & Waffles only uses social media to promote the restaurant. Michael takes all the photos, and he's proud of the fact that they are so well-received. "Waffles make excellent subjects," Michael says with a smile. "They're always beautiful."

In addition to growing the business, Peace, Love, & Waffles would love to set up a gift shop with items inspired by Michael's mom. It's his hope that, along with the mouth-watering waffles they serve, tems with the peace and love theme would bring more visitors to their community. "Dover-Foxcroft has been unfairly skipped over," Michael says. "Although I'm not from here, I've fallen in love with the area. This is a place where people can escape the stresses of everyday life, and Peace, Love, & Waffles can be an oasis where folks can just relax and be happy." Relaxed, happy, and full of delicious waffles.

———◦•◆•◦———

OPEN YEAR ROUND
Wednesday thru Sunday 7:00 a.m. to 2:00 p.m.
207-564-7700

Spring Creek BBQ

26 Greenville Road
MONSON

I t was Mike's lemonade that brought Mike and Kim Witham together.

The couple met at a bluegrass festival 25 years ago. Kim was cranking out hot fajitas at the festival, when Mike, who was selling barbeque, offered her one of his special lemonades. "He saw that I was feeling stressed," Kim says. "And the lemonade really helped!" It was that special lemonade that won Kim over.

When the festival season ended, Mike and Kim wintered together in a rustic camp and came out engaged. Soon after getting married, the couple decided to open a restaurant. In 1999, Mike and Kim opened their first brick and mortar place in Monson, population 700. "Monson's gone through a big transformation these last few years," Kim says.

The restaurant, a barn-style building located next to their home, is decorated with fun chalkboard signs, like the couple's "web address"; *www.comesitontheporchandtalktous. com* and their seasonal hours, "Hit or miss. On a whim. By appointment."

Staying afloat in such a small town can be challenging, and each season brings a different clientele. Hunting season brings people in during the fall, and snowmobilers populate the restaurant in the winter. Spring is when people come to town to open their camps or look for new properties to buy, and summer, their busiest season, welcomes hikers from the Appalachian Trail.

Spring Creek BBQ's best sellers include the most tender pork ribs and pork sandwiches with Kim's amazing cornbread. Mike roasts brisket and makes his own pastrami that he pairs with Morse's Sauerkraut. Other favorites are macaroni and cheese and seasonal desserts baked fresh by Kim, like carrot cake or strawberry rhubarb pie.

"Our goal is to make delicious, homemade, comfort food the Maine way," Kim says. "Maine is all about a simpler way of life and we embrace that. We enjoy preparing good food for our patrons and then welcome the chance to sit on the porch and connect with them."

———◦•◆•◦———

Open Thursday thru Sunday,
Noon to 7:00 p.m.
*They only accept cash, so be sure to visit
an ATM before arriving.*
207-997-7025

Turning Page Farm

842 N. Guilford Rd.
MONSON

Deer, goats, and cheese? You must be in Monson! Tim and Joy are living their passion on their quaint farm as they expand on the knowledge they gained while living in Munich, Germany. Tim brews exceptional beers while Joy lovingly cares for the goats that will produce the creamy, rich milk used to make her delicious herbed artisanal cheeses.

Diners will enjoy German sausages, artisanal cheeses, and belly-warming food like Joy's famous four-cheese mac and cheese. Pair a sausage with Tim's Red Ale and enjoy watching the goats living it up in the pen next to the open-air dining pavilion.

Goat school? Why, yes, indeed! Not only can you bottle feed and frolic with these cute kids, but, you can enjoy a two-day course that will have you ready to run your own goat farm.

We're not kid-ding. :)

OPEN SATURDAY AND SUNDAY
Noon to 6:00 p.m.
207-876-6360

Café Crepe Food Truck

37 Pritham Avenue
GREENVILLE

Lauren Brinkmann grew up in the restaurant world, with her French mom as her teacher. After opening restaurants that she would then have to leave due to her husband's job reassignment, her mom realized that she needed a solution. While Lauren explored the slopes of Colorado, her mom experimented with a food truck business. She sold her delicious crepes in North Carolina at farmer's markets and festivals.

Lauren, a self-professed ski bum, needed something to do to make a living. Seeing how lucrative the food truck business was, while allowing time for Lauren's passion for skiing, she opened her own food truck in Breckenridge in the winter of 2010. A Summer of wine festivals, beer festivals, and hot air balloon festivals with her crepe truck followed.

In 2012, Lauren and

her mom both moved to Greenville, Maine and opened a food truck together. Two years later, Lauren decided to try out the festivals in Southern Maine and even opened a brick-and-mortar location in Freeport. After a few years, Lauren realized that she missed the food truck and its simplicity, so back to Greenville she went.

Cafe Crepe is now in its eleventh season with Lauren at the counter making crepes and talking with her community. "Everyone has a story about their first crepe," Lauren says. It's a connection with her customers that she really enjoys. "People always ask if I eat crepes anymore. I love what I do. I sometimes eat one or two crepes a day!"

Lauren's savory crepe, The Roma, filled with mozzarella, tomato, olive spread, spinach, and pesto is her best seller of the savory variety. "The Club, which is piled high with ham, turkey, cheddar cheese, tomato, spinach and chipotle mayo, is right up there, too," says Lauren. "After I make it, I give it a quick griddle to melt the cheese and provide a finished crepe that's nice and crisp." When you think of crepes, strawberry, or Nutella come to mind. Cafe Crepe has those sweet crepes, too, but, with a twist! The Monkey Bee, filled with Nutella, bananas, and honey is a favorite, as is the Strawberry Cheesecake with lush strawberries, sweet cream, and graham crackers. Lauren offers a gluten free and dairy free as well. There is something for everyone and her delicious crepe concoctions make it difficult to decide!

Now, with two kids of her own, Lauren enjoys the simplicity of running a food truck. Her mom does the behind-the-scenes prep work, allowing Lauren to spend time experimenting with her kids in her home kitchen after the food truck closes each day.

With a 7- x 12-foot truck, Lauren is impressed by what she can do in such a tiny space. She has the perfect amount of room to create her crepes, fresh iced tea, iced coffee, and iced lemonade. "It's tiny. It's small. It's simple," says Lauren. "And I love it!"

OPEN SEASONALLY
Wednesday thru Saturday,
10:00 a.m. to 3:00 p.m.
970-389-8677

Chase Farm Bakery

333 Townhouse Road
WHITEFIELD

If you drive on the scenic roads in Whitefield, don't be surprised if you see an Amish buggy or two. Robin Chase was instrumental in bringing the Amish to the community. She then housed families of Amish on her farm and hired the young girls to help in her kitchen.

Robin and her husband purchased Chase Farm in 1975 and started with milking cows and selling raw milk in Bell canning jars. As she waited for the empty jar returns, she had excess milk to use, so she decided to bake with it. She thought selling her fresh baked treats at the local farmer's markets could be a viable income, however, she knew she couldn't get in on baked goods alone. Thankfully, Robin had luck getting into the markets with her raw milk and homemade butter. In winter, when the market was slow, she made ricotta cheese, Greek yogurt, mozzarella, and about 200 pounds of butter so the milk did not get wasted.

Twenty-five years ago, she started the Chase Farm Bakery. Waking at 2:00 a.m., she would start baking. With their Amish carts parked out front, the young ladies worked with Robin until it was time to marry and build their own homes. They helped Robin make donuts, pies, cookies, biscuits, whoopie pies, English muffins, cinnamon buns, breads, corn bread, scones, and galettes. They would work until about 6:00 p.m. preparing wholesale orders for restaurants, stores, and the nearby orchard. Tuesday and Thursday were delivery days, first to Gardiner, then Hallowell, and finally Augusta. They would then reload and go to Damariscotta, Weatherbird, and the orchard. "The girls are almost all grown now," Robin says

wistfully. I only have one helper on Wednesday and another Amish girl one day a week."

After hiring two additional employees, Robin's bakery is thriving. "The restaurant in town gets 65 to 70 loaves of bread per week," Robin says, "and I make about 500 donuts daily." Robin said she never could have found a way to make that many donuts if it wasn't for the machine, fondly called "The Donut Robot," that Robin purchased a few years back. "I was able to tweak my donut recipe so that it flowed through the Donut Robot, into the oil, and onto the conveyor belt." Now she can make 300 warm, crispy donuts an hour!

The farm also raises cattle and pigs in order to sell ground beef and sausage. Robin laughs, "The pigs love donuts and are not very happy if they don't get warm donuts with their breakfast."

Besides the Donut Robot, Robin's most prized possession is her "Bakery Bible." She compiled all the recipes that she has created and tweaked over the years. "I'm self-taught and a scratch baker," Robin says proudly. "I don't make anything that I don't personally love. And I *LOVE* Donuts!"

———◦•◆•◦———

Open Wednesday thru Saturday
7:00 a.m. to 5:00 p.m.
207-549-7611

Sterlingtown Public House

289 Common Road
UNION

Perched at the top of a hill with views across the valley of a neighboring farm to the south and the town square to the east, lies the Sterlingtown Public House, where the food is anything but pub grub and the hosts have roots steeped in the community. Brian Fickett and his wife Jillian (Lary) are proud and excited to be continuing to plant roots, as his great aunt and great grandmother did before him.

The Public House is located next to what used to be Susabels, a successful retail clothing business on the Village Common in Union his aunt and grandmother opened. Susabel's was a landmark in Union for locals and visitors alike for almost forty years. "In a sense, things have come full circle" Brian says, "bringing our family back to the Union Common."

With a charming outdoor dining area, the atmosphere is as vibrant as the food. "Good food is approachable," Brian says. "We classify our public house offerings as sophisticated comfort. It is in our nature to take something traditional and make it our own, make it unexpectedly good so it's memorable. We also emphasize fresh, scratch-made, local ingredients."

The evidence is in their delicious Bang Bang Mushrooms; so good that mushroom haters become mushroom lovers! Their Thai Peanut Rice Bowl is a gluten-free favorite. While they last, Brian's great aunt's famous Abbot squares (both the famous Abbot squares and Abbot Way in Union are named for Brian's beloved aunt) can be found on the pub's dessert menu along with cakes and cookies.

Family is incredibly important to Brian and Jillian. Although it's just the two of them working and growing this beautiful business and hub of their community, Brian states, "We have endless love and support from both sides of the family, and we are super grateful to have both sets of our parents living locally and always able to lend a hand when needed."

Having found such success in the small community of 2,300 residents, Brian and Jillian took the plunge and opened Sterlingtown Bakehouse just down the street. "It all happened so fast," Brian says. "A changing of hands at 30 Burkett opened up the opportunity for us to rent the ground floor. Having already developed business plans for a bakehouse, we had no hesitation. It was a solid two months of blood, sweat, and tears to transform the space into how we envisioned Sterlingtown Bakehouse."

The menu for the bakery is ever changing, and includes sweets, pastries, breads, and savory bites. There is also fresh roasted coffee and a deli case full of grab-and-go items including sandwiches, salads, and sides. A selection of retail craft beer, cider, mead, and wines to take home and enjoy is also available.

Open Wednesday thru Friday, 3:00 to 8:00 p.m.
Saturday, 11:00 a.m. to 8:00 p.m.
Sunday, 11:00 a.m. to 3:00 p.m.
207-785-0037

Sheba's Wicked Kitchen

822 Kennedy Drive
OAKLAND

When Sheila Iverson was a police officer, she had no idea that her nickname, which was gifted to her from a bunch of guys who knew her for her squats as a powerlifter, would inspire a future food truck. As the owner of Sheba's Wicked Kitchen, her former powerlifting skills allow her to carry the 80- to 100-pound cases of pork shoulder for her famous carnitas.

Sheila's love of food started on a 300-acre farm where she grew up in Maine. "If my family did not grow it, we did not eat it," she says. "If we did not milk it, we did not drink it." Sheila's dad was retired military and he loved to cook. Sheila, eager to learn all she could about food and how to prepare it, would pull up a chair and ask to stir the sauce. She eventually learned all the basics, and at every family gathering or party, Sheila was always asked to cook.

One day in August, the idea of a food trailer just popped into her head. By November, the truck was in her barn. She grabbed the bull by the

horns and Sheba's Wicked Kitchen opened to serve elevated street fare.

Sticking to the focus on quality and freshness that she learned growing up, nothing from Sheba's Wicked Kitchen comes out of a can. Everything she serves is from a fresh source. She makes her own buttermilk ranch with a fresh avocado. Believing simple is better, Sheila makes a fresh sweet and tangy mango salsa with ripe juicy mangoes and just the right amount of spice.

Sheila believes the main element of any good food is rustic, and that simple is better. Her dishes are crafted in small batches and always fresh. That was the focus when she created her first menu item, a fish taco. Using fresh Maine haddock, the fish is lightly breaded and fried to a golden brown. These are served on three warm flour tortillas (corn tortillas for gluten-free folks), then topped with mango salsa, chipotle crema, and purple cabbage. Her slow-roasted pork carnita tacos are her most popular, combining pork roasted for twelve hours, proprietary rustic Mexican spices which are layered with grilled red onion, avocado, chipotle crema, and fresh cilantro, and served in either flour or corn tortillas.

<hr>

OPEN SEASONALLY, SOMETIMES AS LATE AS JANUARY
Offers vegan, vegetarian, and gluten-free options.
Wednesday thru Friday, 3:00 to 8:00 p.m.
Saturday, 11:00 a.m. to 8:00 p.m.
Sunday, 11:00 a.m. to 3:00 p.m.
In September, Hours Change: Friday, 11:00 a.m. to 4:00 p.m.
Saturday and Sunday, 11:00 a.m. to 3:00 p.m

THE FARMER'S DAUGHTER

13 Rumford Rd
Oquossoc, Maine

In the town of Rangeley lies the tiny village of Oquossoc. Known for the beauty of Rangeley Lake, the plenitude of hiking and the vast array of cross-country skiing, snowshoeing, and snowmobile trails, this little village seems to have everything for the outdoor enthusiast.

Foodies also have reason to be excited! This spot is a paradise of fresh fruits and vegetables, delicious crusty breads, local jams, maple syrup, beer, wine, gourmet foods and so many amazing cheeses! The literal cream on the top is the homemade ice cream served from an open window out front. Cold creamy concoctions like Espresso Crunch, Graham Central, and Chocolate Explosion will excite kids of all ages.

OPEN DAILY MEMORIAL DAY WEEKEND THROUGH LABOR DAY

9:00 a.m. to 5:00 p.m.
Sometimes longer if the weather holds.

Puzzle Mountain Bakery

806 Bear River Road
NEWRY

Ten minutes north of Bethel sits a little bakery stand owned by Ryan and Devon Wheeler. People from all over the world stop at the end of their driveway to buy pies. Ryan's mom Mary Jo Kelly started Puzzle Mountain Bakery in 1999, but her interest was in pottery rather than pies. A potter in Bethel, she had read somewhere that the way to sell pie plates was to fill them with pies, so she did. It turned out, folks were coming more for the pies than the plates, so she shifted her energy to baking.

Ryan, in the meantime, had his own landscaping company, but wound up helping his mom quite a bit in the kitchen. Besides working in a few Maine restaurants and pizzerias from time to time, Ryan learned everything he knows from his mom. In 2010, when Mary Jo retired, Ryan took over.

Ryan's wife Devon, who went to fashion school, hadn't spent much time in the kitchen. But since baking was such a big part of Ryan's life, she wanted to learn as much as she could. Together, they grew the bakery, and their volume exploded. "The amount of pies we sell in a day is the same as what we sold in an entire week when my mom ran it," Ryan says.

Part of that increase in volume is due to the fact that Puzzle Mountain Bakery started out as a passer-by bakery. People would stop if they saw it, but now it's become a destination bakery. "We do get quite a few locals, but we see a lot more tourists," Devon says. "We meet so many customers who tell us they drove from Massachusetts or Rhode Island, just to buy some pies."

Open May 1 through December 1, the change of seasons brings a change of customers. "Our busiest season is summer, of course, but the foliage season comes a close second," Ryan says. "We also see skiers in December. The population here seems to have increased significantly in the past two years. So many more folks have bought ski homes!"

The stand also sees Canadians heading to Southern Maine for vacations. "We accept Canadian currency at the bakery," Ryan says. "Then when we have enough Canadian money, we cross the border and take our son to the zoo. We love spending time in Canada. It's so close, but it's like a different world."

Wild Maine blueberry is their best-selling pie, but maple cream cookies are probably their bestseller. Puzzle Mountain Bakery only sells a few items: fruit pies, a maple cream cookie, chocolate whoopie pies, and their own homemade jam. "We'll do seasonal items like pumpkin pie or chocolate maple cream whoopie pies," Devon says. "But those core items are our staples. Customers can always count on seeing them at the stand."

Puzzle Mountain Bakery only uses Down East wild blueberries for their jam and pies. "We love the wild Maine blueberries," Ryan says, "and our customers love them too. They're sweeter, they make a better pie, and you get more fruit in a pie

than the bigger blueberries. Plus, you get an authentic Maine flavor!"

Puzzle Mountain Bakery relies on the honor system so customers can help themselves and leave their money behind. "It's such a big part of the experience," Ryan says.

"People from big cities are especially taken with the honor system," Devon adds. "They're blown away that the honor system, overall, actually works. They tell us that would never happen in New York City." Although theft is sometimes inevitable, they have taken precautions, and it took them a little while to find the right money box. "We've gone through a lot of money boxes through the years, with people trying to steal them or use a hammer to smash them open," Ryan says. "Now we use a big, old air tank from an old mining company that my grandfather used to have. It's a big metal tank filled with concrete, with a little slot people can put their money in." Of course, there is still theft, but they've "baked" that into the business. "Although theft has grown significantly over the last two years, we're trying to keep the honor system and trust alive," Devon says. "We've been doing this for twenty-five years, and we know there will be issues," Ryan adds. "But there are a lot more good people than bad people, and some folks actually pay more than they owe to help us offset that. We're very thankful for those people, because they help make up for the people who don't do the right thing, and that keeps our business alive."

"We like to keep our overhead low," Ryan says. "Because we don't have to have a big, air-conditioned store with staff at the counter, we can pass our savings along to our customers. When people don't pay for pies, especially now with inflation so high, it makes it harder for us to be able to do that."

Puzzle Mountain Bakery just started to accept Venmo. "We were never able to do anything like that prior," Ryan says, "because we didn't have any cell phone service up here before!" Since cell phone service can be spotty, customers sometimes have to take their goodies and Venmo later when they get home.

The stand is filled all day long, with any leftover items coming in at sunset. "Customers will come at all hours," Ryan says, "and if they don't see anything at the stand, they'll walk up the driveway to the house."

Literally a "mom and pop store," Devon and Ryan run the stand full-time by themselves. They're also parents of a

six-year-old with another one on the way. "We've grown so
much that sometimes it's hard to keep up," Devon says, with
Ryan adding "Baking pies takes many long hours. We have no
weekends or holidays off in the summer, but it's worth it."

They're especially proud that their son can see how that
process works. He puts price stickers on the cookies, and sometimes helps in the kitchen. Devon and Ryan spend all of their
time together, working five days a week in the bakery and
spending their days off together as well. "We spend almost all
of our time together," Devon says. "But it works out well."

Devon and Ryan are hoping to continue baking and
passing the tradition down to their own kids. "It's more of a
lifestyle than a job," Ryan says. "Spending that much time on
your feet and using your hands can be physically grueling.

Everything is rolled out by hand. The shortening in the pie crust is cut in by hand, rather than by mixer, to make the dough flakier. "My mom had to retire because she developed carpal tunnel." Ryan said, "but as long as our bodies work, so will we!"

———⬥———

OPEN DAILY MAY THRU SEPTEMBER

DOLCE AMICI GELATO & COCKTAILS

427 Main Street
NORWAY

When you see a gelato sign in this sweet little town, you immediately pull over, because . . . gelato! Exciting Italian flavors await the opportunity to tease your tastebuds; Coconut or Coffee Stracciatella, Dairy Free Lemon Sorbetto or Pistachio. The bonus at Dolce Amici is the delicious fresh sandwiches, salads, and unique custom cocktails that you can either enjoy inside or al fresco. Fun for the family, or a really great date night.

OPEN YEAR ROUND

Wednesday, Noon to 7:00 p.m.
Thursday, Noon to 8:00 p.m.
Sunday, 10:00 a.m. to 3:00 p.m.
207-743-3900

Sticky Sweet

119 Cumberland Avenue
PORTLAND

While Portland is not exactly, "out of the way," there's not a good chance that folks will find Sticky Sweet by accident. Tucked away in a mostly residential neighborhood, most of Sticky Sweet's customers intentionally seek out the shop that serves only plant-based ice cream.

A vegetarian for over a decade, Ashley Dow watched the documentary *Forks Over Knives* and became vegan overnight. She decided it was the best diet for her health, animals, and the environment, but didn't want to give up the foods she loved and grew up on. "When I became vegan, I found a new passion," Ashley says. "I became obsessed with recreating my favorite dishes, so I started cooking and experimenting." Since Ashley's favorite foods included rich, creamy fare like maca-roni and cheese and ice cream, she knew she had to find a way to get that creamy flavor into her food. Using nuts and nut

butters, Ashley created her first
ice cream flavor: sea salted maple.

In an effort to keep the ice
cream not only vegan but as
healthy as possible, Ashley uses
fresh, whole ingredients. Sea
salted maple, for instance, only
has four ingredients: coconut
milk, cashews, sea salt, and maple
sugar.

Shortly after Ashley became
vegan, her sister Kelley followed.
The two opened a small stall at Portland's Public Market
House where they sold only three flavors: sea salted maple,
blueberry, and cinnamon sugar cookie. Ashley figured that
she'd one day expand into other vegan desserts, and it wasn't
until one of their regular customers suggested they open a
scoop shop that just focuses on ice cream that they even enter-
tained the idea. "She said that our ice cream is so good, it
should be all we do." That was the seed for Sticky Sweet.

After looking at retail spaces throughout the city in 2018,
Ashley and Kelley decided on Portland's East End. At the
time, a few breweries were opening up, and it seemed to be an
up-and-coming neighborhood for foodie spots. They found a
place they liked, but it was being rented out as an apartment.
The landlord agreed to lease it as a commercial space, so,
doing the work themselves, they gutted it and reconfigured it
as a scoop shop.

"We had no idea how the shop would be received," Ashley
said. "We're vegans, but it's not like we have a big community

of vegan friends and family." It turns out the reception was hugely positive. Most of Sticky Sweet's customers are not vegan, but rather, they are staying away from dairy or gluten because of allergies, health reasons, animal welfare, or to be environmentally friendly. "Many of our customers are knowledgeable about the benefits of a plant-based diet, but they don't want to go one hundred percent," Ashley says. "Because we offer ice cream that tastes really good, they say they can at least make that change and feel happy about it."

Customers agree that, vegan or not, Sticky Sweet's ice cream is simply incredible. With flavors like Butter Pecan Praline, Key Lime Pie, Funky Monkey, Dark Chocolate Peppermint, and Chocolate Cream Pie (to name just a few), Ashley and Kelley are thrilled that customers not only feel good about eating their ice cream, but they rave that it's even more decadent than ice cream made with dairy.

Sticky Sweet was open for a season when the pandemic hit. "We had to close the scoop shop down, but we opened a

take-out window," Ashley says. "Then, when things started to open up again, we had grown so much that we had to bring in more freezers to accommodate that growth. Soon, the scoop shop was filled with freezers!" Sticky Sweet is looking to relocate to a bigger location, in order to expand and bring people back together inside again. Another benefit of a larger location is that Ashley will be able to experiment with seed-based ice cream so people with nut allergies will have options as well.

"That's something I'm committed to doing in the near future," she says. "I'd love to create delicious options for everyone."

Because of the high-quality ingredients, Sticky Sweet is a bit pricier than other ice cream shops. "Unlike a lot of vegan ice creams out there that are using artificial thickeners or stabilizers or gums, we're using cashews and other real whole foods, " says Ashley. "We're not watering our ice cream down. The only sweeteners we use are dates, local maple, organic coconut sugar, or organic cane sugar. We charge a premium price only to be able to cover our costs." Sticky Sweet is fortunate that most of their customers know that, and they don't balk at the prices. They understand and appreciate the value of real whole foods.

Even with the higher prices, Ashley and Kelley do not yet draw a salary. "It's a labor of love," Ashley says. "That's why we keep going. We know our customers love our ice cream and we feel good about the fact that we're making something really great, both in taste and in quality."

All of the ice cream is made from scratch using raw ingredients, as are the brownies, cookies, and chips that get mixed into the ice cream. "The only thing we bake are the ice cream cones, which are all gluten-free," Ashley says.

Sticky Sweet is a family business. Ashley and Kelly's brother recently left his job at a bakery to work at the shop full time, and their dad and stepmom recently moved up from Texas to help out as they've gotten busier. In addition to the ice cream shop, Sticky Sweet also sells hand-packed pints in eighteen Maine stores.

Prior to Sticky Sweet, Kelley was working in the insurance industry and Ashley, who has a Masters of Social Work, was working for a non-profit organization. "Becoming vegan sparked a brand new passion for me," Ashley says. "I was meant to make vegan food."

———◦•◆•◦———

SUMMER HOURS:
Wednesday thru Sunday, 2:00 p.m. to 9:00 p.m.

OFF-SEASON HOURS:
Thursday thru Friday, 4:00 p.m. to 8:00 p.m.
Saturday & Sunday, 2:00 p.m. to 8:00 p.m.

JOHN'S ICE CREAM FACTORY

510 Belfast Augusta Road
LIBERTY

John Ascrizzi has been in the ice cream business since the 1970s. It's a must-stop on Route 3 as you head toward Augusta. So many creamy flavors of delicious, small batch, premium home-made ice cream makes it hard to choose! Peanut butter crunch, ginger, chocolate coconut almond, and the creamiest most deliciously simple flavor, vanilla, to name a few.

Originally from Long Island, John's father had a pasta manufacturing business. John could be seen working along-side his dad, making authentic pastas like ravioli and tortel-lini. After the family business sold and they moved to Florida, John started working in an ice cream franchise with his sister and brother-in-law. He eventually purchased the ice cream shop and ran it until 1998, when he heard the call of Maine.

John's Ice Cream Factory is a favorite stop for locals and tourists alike who pull off Route 3 to try creamy scoops of ice cream on crunchy cones, or great big sundaes with a choice of toppings. The ice cream cakes can be customized with your favorite flavors of ice cream and layers of chocolate, caramel, fruits . . . or anything else you can dream up!

John's brings out the child in all of us as we wait in line and think to ourselves, "I scream, you scream, we ALL scream for ice cream!"

OPEN YEAR ROUND
Tuesday thru Sunday
Noon to 7:00 p.m.

The Love Card

This little Maine nugget is not food for the belly, but rather, food for the soul. In writing this book, it was amazing to see the hurdles each business endured to stay afloat as we navigated unprecedented situations due to a worldwide pandemic. The message that kept repeating was love and support. Love from families and friends. Love and support from the surrounding community.

When Momo's Cheesecakes ran into a supply chain issue that left them without the main ingredient for their cakes, a customer emailed them. He said, "I am in Pennsylvania on my way to Maine. I will stop at every store along the way and buy all their cream cheese." When The Scone Goddess had to ration raspberries because of the shortage, customers offered bags of frozen berries they had harvested from their own gardens. When there was a staff shortage, families rallied to support the businesses of their loved ones. The community showed up. They bought local, supported the business with their wallets, and gave gratitude and praise of the businesses to their friends.

Family. Friends. Community. Love. These are 4 Maine ingredients found in the pages we wrote. With that in mind, we invite you to read the story of The Love Card, one simple paper card that is reaching the hearts of people across the globe.

Feel free to check out Love Cards at https://www.thelove-card.org.

THE LOVE CARD MISSION: "To spread love to as many people on the planet as possible and to empower others to do the same. Since 2016, we have given away over 250,000 Love Cards. Anyone who wants free Love Cards can have them. It is our hope that this pay-it-forward movement grows and reminds people of the power of love."

Life is not easy.

Let's try to help each soul we meet.

Each of us is doing our best with what we have been given.

Let go of judgment.

Love each other.

You'll never really know how much someone needed your love in that moment.

~Joanne LaCarrubba Steenberg
Penobscot, Maine

Acknowledgments

RONNI ARNO

Thank you to Josh, Hallie, and Morgan, for their unwavering support and always picking up my slack when I'm on deadline! Thank you to my co-author Veronica, whose enthusiasm for this project was contagious. Thank you to our editor Michael Steere and to Down East Books for believing in this project. The biggest thank you goes out to the folks featured in this book, and to all the Mainers who make the Pine Tree State so special, loveable, and downright delicious.

VERONICA STUBBS

A huge thank you to my family, Jason, Riah, Andy, and Izzi, for the encouragement to always follow my dreams. Gratitude to my co-author, Ronni and her "Let's do it!" attitude. To all of YOU, thank you for supporting Maine's amazing small businesses and appreciating the love, passion, and huge amount of effort it takes to survive and thrive. We so love and appreciate you!